100 QUESTIONS about OCEANS

and all
the answers
too!

Written and Illustrated by
Simon Abbott

 PETER PAUPER PRESS, INC.
White Plains, New York

PETER PAUPER PRESS

In 1928, at the age of twenty-two, Peter Beilenson began printing books on a small press in the basement of his parents' home in Larchmont, New York. Peter—and later, his wife, Edna—sought to create fine books that sold at "prices even a pauper could afford."

Today, still family owned and operated, Peter Pauper Press continues to honor our founders' legacy of quality, value, and fun for big kids and small kids alike.

For Dora, Tabby, Jack, Ray, and Oscar

Designed by Heather Zschock

Text and illustrations copyright © 2019 by Simon Abbott

Published by Peter Pauper Press, Inc.
202 Mamaroneck Avenue
White Plains, New York 10601 USA

Published in the United Kingdom and Europe by Peter Pauper Press, Inc.
c/o White Pebble International
Unit 2, Plot 11 Terminus Rd.
Chichester, West Sussex PO19 8TX, UK

Library of Congress Cataloging-in-Publication Data Available

ISBN 978-1-4413-2939-4
Manufactured for Peter Pauper Press, Inc.
Printed in Hong Kong

7 6 5 4 3 2 1

Visit us at www.peterpauper.com

Let's explore the ocean depths
and discover the wonders
beneath the waves!

Dive into breathtaking coral reefs teeming
with life and mysterious deep trenches filled
with weird and wonderful specimens.

Which fish is the fastest swimmer?

How big are the colossal squid's
gigantic eyes?

Why does a flying fish fly?
(Try saying that ten times in a row!)

It's time to get up close and personal with
some sensational sea creatures and begin
our journey to a world under the sea!

OCEANS ALIVE!

Let's begin with a look at Planet Earth and get familiar with our five fantastic oceans. Take the plunge, and uncover some surprising statistics!

How much of the planet is underwater?
An amazing 70% of the Earth's surface is covered by oceans. About 97% of all the planet's water can be found in its seas!

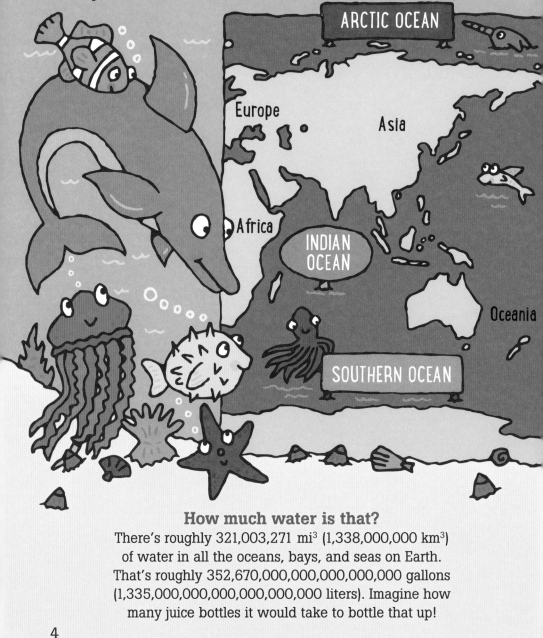

ARCTIC OCEAN

Europe

Asia

Africa

INDIAN OCEAN

Oceania

SOUTHERN OCEAN

How much water is that?
There's roughly 321,003,271 mi³ (1,338,000,000 km³) of water in all the oceans, bays, and seas on Earth. That's roughly 352,670,000,000,000,000,000 gallons (1,335,000,000,000,000,000,000 liters). Imagine how many juice bottles it would take to bottle that up!

Wow! So, is there enough space for the millions of marine creatures?
Sure! The oceans take up about 99% of the habitable space on this planet, so they have plenty of elbow room.

Which ocean is the biggest?
It's the Pacific Ocean, which is larger than the total land area of Earth!

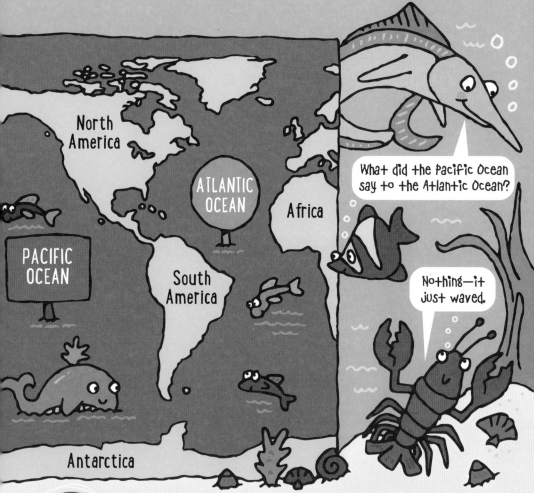

Is the bottom of the ocean a flat, sandy surface?
Not at all! From what explorers have discovered so far, the sea floor is a jumble of ridges, trenches, pillars, chimneys, mountain ranges, and even bubbling underwater volcanoes.

"So far"? Are there are parts of the ocean that are unexplored?
We've only investigated a tiny 5% of the Earth's oceans. Amazingly, we know more about the surface of Mars than we do of the ocean floor.

MAKING WAVES

Shall we float back to the beginning? Let's see how our oceans began, and say "hello" to the prehistoric creatures still making a splash today!

How old are the oceans?

Our ancient seas first formed about 3.8 billion years ago. As Earth's molten rocks gradually cooled, water vapor escaped and fell as rain. This water washed into the Earth's craters and cavities and became an ocean.

What are some of the first sea creatures still bobbing around today?

A jellyfish called the **comb jelly** has been drifting through the oceans for an incredible 500 million years. The 450 million-year-old **horseshoe crab** gets a special mention too.

SURVIVORS CLUB!

What other ancient sea creatures are still making a splash under the surface?

Take a look on the side of your bathtub. Scientists believe that **sea sponges** were the first animal to appear on Earth, clocking up an impressive 640 million years on the planet. In the fish world, the **lamprey** is a 300 million-year-old scary specimen.

Which prehistoric sea-going specimens bid farewell to life on Earth? Let's cast our net and catch some extinct examples. The 40-foot (12 m) long **Thalassomedon** had huge eyes and a long, thin neck. This was ideal when hunting for groups of unsuspecting fish swimming above their heads.

The **Mosasaurus** terrorized the prehistoric seas, powering through the water with its shark-like tail and formidable flippers. This beast was longer than a school bus and three times the weight of an average African elephant!

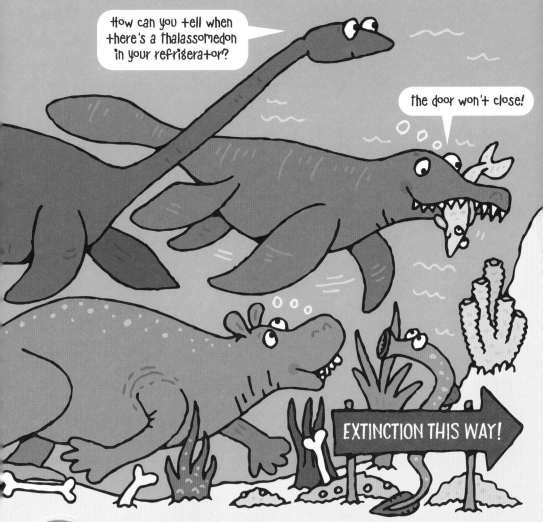

How can you tell when there's a thalassomedon in your refrigerator?

the door won't close!

EXTINCTION THIS WAY!

FACT OR FICTION

Were all prehistoric creatures bloodthirsty meat eaters? Not at all! Take a look at the **Desmostylian**. This hippo-sized mammal swam like a polar bear and used its unusual snout and jaw to slurp up vegetation like a vacuum cleaner.

THE SPLASH ZONE SEARCH

Finish up your ice-cream and rub on some sunscreen. We're going to hit the beach and tiptoe around the tide pools!

What is a tide pool?

At low tide the sea backs away, leaving behind sea water which fills the cavities and hollows in the shoreline's rocks. These are tide, or rock, pools.

What creatures would I find there?

Take some time, and try to watch an **anemone** in action. They use their tentacles to catch small snails, fish, and tiny organisms called plankton, then pop their prey into their central mouths. You might spot **barnacles**, **clams**, **snails**, **limpets**, and **mussels** stuck onto the rocks, too.

How do these creatures protect themselves?

Let's take mussels as an example. They develop hard shells that can thicken if a predator comes near. The shell will also protect the creature from drying out when exposed to the sun and wind at low tide. Mussels attach themselves to rocks, which stops the waves from washing them away and makes picking them off harder for predators.

Which tide pool terrors should I try to avoid?
Rock pool residents such as the **hermit crab** and **striped shore crab** shouldn't do you any harm, but I'd steer clear of the **coconut crab**. The front claws of this crustacean can pinch with the same force as an adult lion's jaw. Dodge the **sea urchin**, too. These spike-covered sea creatures have a nasty sting, especially when touched or trodden on.

What did one tide pool say to the other tide pool?

Show me your mussels!

Striped Shore Crab

Hermit Crab

Coconut Crab

Snail

What do the tide pool inhabitants themselves need to watch out for?
Their main predators are hungry sea otters, sea birds, and fish. It's not all bad news though. If a **starfish** loses an arm to a sea otter, it just grows a replacement. That's handy!

Let's move along the beach to the sandy shore. What could we spot as we search the coast line? **Sand crabs** are egg-shaped critters that can grow up to 1.5" (3.8 cm) long. They are claw-less and survive by eating the plankton caught in their antennae. Sensible **beach hoppers** escape the heat of the day by digging holes under wet sand. **Bloodworms** eat sand as they dig, and consider anything that fits in their mouths along with the sand, food.

We're getting closer to the sea. What is this area called? **Mudflats**. These areas are often found in sheltered places, such as bays and lagoons. Mud is deposited here by the tides, and it's a popular spot for hungry seabirds.

Do any sea species live down on the mudflats? Of course! Many of these creatures are called **filter feeders**, which means they strain particles or small organisms out of the seawater to survive. Clams, oysters, and cockles are examples of filter feeders that live on the shoreline.

Which other creatures call the mudflats home?
Here comes the **pink ghost shrimp**. This shoreline resident lives
in a maze of underground tunnels, with openings that look like
mini-volcanoes. It shares its tunnels with small clams, pea crabs,
and marine worms.

**Which are
the most common
creatures on the mudflat?**
It's hard to say, but my vote would
go to the humble **lugworm**. Up to 820,000
of these creatures can be found per acre.

**What's the most important thing
to remember when enjoying a
shoreline search?**
Stay safe! Beaches are a lot of
fun, but strong currents, riptides,
and some sea species can make
them dangerous places.
Put on your sunscreen, pop
on a hat, and stay with
a grown-up. They can
pay for the ice cream too!

SCOUTING OUT THE SWAMPS

Time to get the low-down on life among the mangroves and marshes!

What is a mangrove?

It's a tree growing along the coastal shores in warm, tropical locations. A **marsh** (where mangroves usually are) is an area near the sea that is flooded at high tide by salt water.

How do mangrove forests survive in salty water?

These tough trees live in water 100 times saltier than regular plants. Some mangroves can filter out about 90% of the salt as the sea water enters its roots. Other species sweat the salt out through their leaves, and others store the salt in old leaves or bark, which then fall off or die.

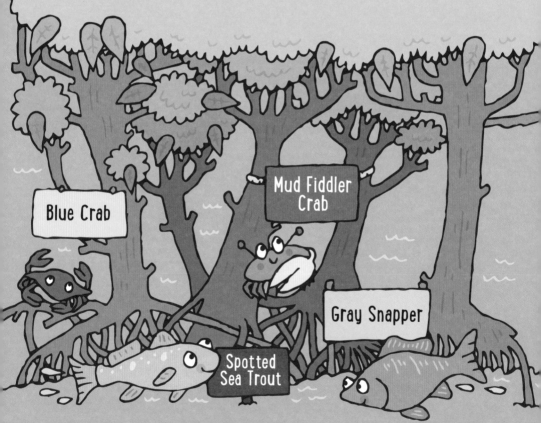

Blue Crab

Mud Fiddler Crab

Gray Snapper

Spotted Sea Trout

Which animals make their home among the mangroves?

These muddy marshes are crawling with life. Let's hear it for the **blue crab, mud fiddler crab**, the **grass shrimp**, the **Atlantic ribbed mussel**, the **spotted sea trout**, and the **gray snapper**, to name just a few!

How do animals adapt to the tidal changes in salt water marshes? Let's look at the humble **oyster**. At low tide, these creatures are surrounded by water with low salt content, so they close their shells, stop feeding, and change their breathing. Hours later, at high tide, the oysters open their shells to feed and breathe in the salty, oxygen-rich water.

Why don't oysters give to charity?

Because they're shellfish!

Who's the salt marsh king? That prize goes to the **American alligator**. This 1,000 lb (450 kg) reptile uses its powerful jaws to snack on anything that gets in its way. Turtles, fish, snakes, and small mammals are often on the menu.

FACT OR FICTION

Do mermaids still secretly splash around in the salt marshes? No, and they never did! This myth is a case of mistaken identity with the **manatee**, a mammal often found on the southeast coast of North America. From a distance, these creatures could be mistaken for humans.

SUPERSTARS OF THE SEA

Let's take the plunge and discover the winners beneath the waves! Who are the outstanding ocean champions?

Who grabs the prize for the biggest sea-going specimen?
Make way for the **blue whale**! It's over twice as long as a school bus, and its tongue alone is as heavy as an elephant.

Have you ever seen a fish cry?

POCKET SIZED SHARK

TEENY TURTLE

SMALLEST SEAHORSE

Which creatures win the "Smallest Species" awards?
Grab your rulers and look out for the inch-long (2.5 cm) **pygmy seahorse**, the smallest seahorse, or even the **dwarf lantern shark**, the tiniest shark, which is only half as long as a bowling pin! The smallest starfish is the fingernail-sized **paddle spined seastar**, and the tiniest turtle is the 2-foot (0.6 m) long **Kemp's ridley sea turtle**.

SMALL-SCALE STARFISH

Which fish has hooked the Deep-Sea Diving Diploma?
The spooky **snailfish** was found at a dizzying depth of over 26,000 feet (7,925 m). That's nearly as deep as Mount Everest is tall!

How fast does the quickest creature go?

That record is held by the spectacular **sailfish**, who has clocked speeds of 68 miles (109 km) per hour. It even overtakes the celebrated cheetah, who trots in at a sluggish 64 miles (103 km) per hour!

Which hazardous creature tops the toxic list?

Avoid the **blue ringed octopus**. It's only the size of an adult's hand, but this eight-legged fellow has enough venom to wipe out 26 humans in minutes! Top prize goes to the frightful **box jellyfish**. Each of its 60 terrifying tentacles features 5,000 stinging cells packed with so much venom that its victims often die before they even reach shore.

ECOSYSTEM EXPLORATION

A quarter of all known marine species live in a coral reef. Let's sink beneath the surface and see what we can spot!

What is a coral? Is it an animal? Is it a plant?
Corals are colorful, motionless creatures attached to the ocean floor. Even though corals generally live their lives in one spot like plants, they are animals.

How is a coral reef constructed?
What we call coral is in fact huge numbers of tiny creatures called **polyps**. These polyps have soft bodies and (sometimes) outer limestone skeletons, which attach to rocks or other polyps. Together, the tiny coral animals create big coral structures, which can be up to 10,000 years old!

What creatures shelter among the coral?
The countless species include fish, seahorses, turtles, sharks, eels, crabs, lobster, shrimps, sea urchins, sea snakes, sponges, and algae.

SPOTFIN LIONFISH

Let's take a look at some of the colorful creatures among the coral!

Where is it found? South Pacific and Indian Oceans

How big is it? 18 inches (46 cm), just shorter than a cat!

What should I watch out for? Its venomous spines. These can cause immense pain!

CORAL REEF SNAKE

Where is it found? Indian and Pacific Oceans

How big is it? It can grow up to 5 feet (1.5 m) long.

What should I watch out for? It is venomous...but it's very reluctant to bite!

16

HAWKSBILL TURTLE

Where is it found? Tropical oceans and reefs all around the world

How big is it? About 35 inches (89 cm) long, and weighs about the same as an average 14-year-old!

What does it eat? It snacks on sponges, sea anemones, and jellyfish.

CROWN OF THORNS STARFISH

Where is it found? Pacific and Indian Oceans

How big is it? 14 inches (36 cm). That's about 5 times the size of a tennis ball.

Is it a good guy or a bad guy? Both! It destroys large areas of the reef by devouring coral. On the other hand, it gets rid of fast-growing coral, which gives slow-growing ones a better chance at survival.

CLOWNFISH (OR ANEMONEFISH)

Where is it found? Pacific and Indian Oceans

How big is it? Just 4 inches (10 cm) long.

Did you know…? Clownfish live among stinging anemone, but they're covered in mucus that keeps them from getting stung.

PARROTFISH

Where is it found? Coral reefs worldwide

How big is it? It can get as big as 4 feet (1.2 m), the height of an average 7-year-old!

Is it a good guy or a bad guy? A good guy! It feeds on the algae that could smother and suffocate a coral reef if left to its own devices.

THE RAINFOREST OF THE SEA

Dive in and examine kelp forests, the underwater woodland!

Kelp? What's that?
Kelp is a long, brown, towering plant (or algae), that lives in cool, clear water near the shore, where it can get the sunlight it needs to grow.

Why do sea creatures live in kelp forests?
To eat and to be safe! **Bristle worms**, **prawns**, **snails**, and **brittle stars** nibble on the holdfasts, or the part of the plant that secures the kelp to the seabed. **Sea urchins** even gnaw through the holdfasts, and the kelp gets washed away. Don't worry too much, though. **Sea otters** devour the urchins before they get too carried away!

Who dives into the kelp forests for protection?
Creatures such as **kelp fish**, **rockfish**, and **sunfish** use the kelp canopy as a safeguard against predators and storms. The bright orange female **Garibaldi** often lays her eggs in a sheltered spot among the kelp, in a neat and tidy nest prepared by the male for the happy event!

These tasty fish are bound to attract the attention of hungry hunters. Which predators plunge into the kelp for a mouth-watering meal? **Sea lions**, **harbor seals**, **sea otters**, and even **whales** call in to chase the catch of the day. **Leopard sharks** cruise the depths of the kelp forest, scooping up **innkeeper worms**, **fish eggs**, **bat rays**, and even **octopus**!

How do kelp forests survive a raging, stormy sea?
Like forests on land, storms and natural disasters can tear up the kelp, leaving behind a shredded mess of seaweed on the shoreline. However, kelp is quick to recover, and can grow up to a foot and a half per day. It's not long before the forest is flourishing once more, with the storms just a distant memory!

SCANNING THE SEA BED

Grab your goggles and take a deep breath. It's time to sink a little deeper and scout out the sandy ocean floor.

What is the sandy sea bed made from?
Weather conditions such as rain, wind, waves, and freezing temperatures break down rocks and minerals, like quartz, into tiny grains. Some sand is made up of broken up shells, skeletons, and even black volcanic glass.

Which animals have adapted to life on the sandy ocean floor?
The foot-long (30 cm) **king ragworm** buries itself in the sand, lining the tunnels with its own mucus. The **sea squirt** fixes itself to the ocean floor, catching food that's drifting by with its tentacle-like arms.

What does a clam do for its birthday?

Who gets the "Outstanding Ocean-floor Odd Bod" Prize?
Introducing the **sea cucumber**! These curious creatures can grow to the size of an adult human, and, if threatened, some of them react in a very peculiar way: by shooting their internal organs out of their butts!

It shellabrates!

Which creature wins the "Sea-Bed Squatter" Award?
Once the **giant clam** attaches itself to the sea bed, it's there for life! This four-foot (1.8 m), 400 lb (181 kg) mollusk can live for over 100 years, but it generously shares its shell with billions of algae that live in the clam's tissues.

The gold star for the "Ocean-Bottom Bad Guy" is up for grabs.
Who's paddling to the podium?
A round of applause for the awe-inspiring **angelshark**. This camouflaged
creature buries itself in the sandy ocean floor, and can seize its
unsuspecting prey in a tenth of a second.

What happens to the sea-bed loving sea creatures in a raging storm?
It's not a problem for sharks and other fast-swimming fish, as they can
sense changes in the sea water and make a quick exit. It's a different story
for slow swimmers, or home-loving creatures reluctant to leave their patch.
These creatures get battered by the waves and suffer through a drop in
oxygen and salt levels.

ORDER IN THE OCEANS

Half the Earth's surface is covered by an ocean almost twice as deep as the Grand Canyon. Let's dip our toe into this enormous expanse.

Can we break this huge expanse down into smaller sections?
Sure! Some sea-loving scientists have split it up based on how deep each section is and how much sunlight reaches it.

What's the first section called?
The **Epipelagic** (ep-ee-puh-laj-ik), or **Photic Zone**

How deep does it go?
650 feet (198 m). That's almost as high as the Golden Gate Bridge!

What have scientists called the middle segment?
The **Mesopelagic** (mez-uh-puh-laj-ik), or **Twilight Zone**, because it gets some light but not a ton.

How deep is this section?
3,300 feet (1,006 m)

What is the third section of the open ocean called?
This is the **Bathypelagic** (bath-uh-puh-laj-ik) or **Aphotic Zone**.

How deep does it go?
13,000 feet (3,962 m)
That's half as tall as Mount Everest!

Wow! The Bathypelagic Zone is deep and dark!
Is there anything beneath it?
Yes—just two more zones:

Abyssopelagic (abb-iss-oh-puh-laj-ik) **Zone**
This stretches from the bottom of the Bathypelagic Zone to the ocean floor.

Hadopelagic (had-oh-puh-laj-ik) **Zone**
These are the ocean's trenches, the deepest, darkest parts of the sea.

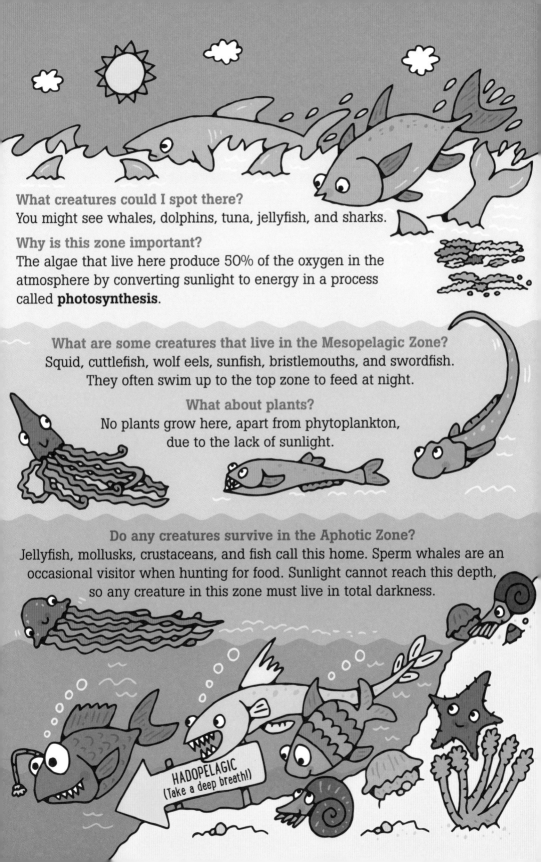

What creatures could I spot there?
You might see whales, dolphins, tuna, jellyfish, and sharks.

Why is this zone important?
The algae that live here produce 50% of the oxygen in the
atmosphere by converting sunlight to energy in a process
called **photosynthesis**.

What are some creatures that live in the Mesopelagic Zone?
Squid, cuttlefish, wolf eels, sunfish, bristlemouths, and swordfish.
They often swim up to the top zone to feed at night.

What about plants?
No plants grow here, apart from phytoplankton,
due to the lack of sunlight.

Do any creatures survive in the Aphotic Zone?
Jellyfish, mollusks, crustaceans, and fish call this home. Sperm whales are an
occasional visitor when hunting for food. Sunlight cannot reach this depth,
so any creature in this zone must live in total darkness.

HADOPELAGIC
(Take a deep breath!)

How do sea creatures exist in this deep-sea desert?
Marine animals use different survival techniques. Let's take a look at a few examples!

What does a 100-foot (30 m), 200-ton blue whale eat?
Their main food source is **krill**, a small ocean-going creature measuring less than an inch.

How many of these bite-sized critters does a blue whale need to snack on?
About 8,000 lbs (3,629 kg) of krill a day.
That's as heavy as a hippo!

TODAY'S SPECIAL

Krill

Does a whale just open its jaw and devour massive groups of krill?
A whale can't digest huge amounts of sea water. Luckily, it has a **baleen plate** hanging down from its upper jaw. These plates are made from keratin (the same stuff found in our fingernails) and look like big combs. They allow the whale to trap krill, filter out sand and salt water, then gobble up the good stuff!

What is blubber?
Fat! A whale can live off hefty stores of blubber for four months.
This is handy for migrating through vast stretches of ocean.

What other features come in handy when out hunting in the open ocean?
Blue marlins are some of the ocean's fastest movers. They have spear-like snouts, which they use to slash their way through schools of unsuspecting fish. Then they turn around and return to gobble up the dazed victims.

Where do flying fish go to borrow money?

How do creatures in the open ocean take cover from predators?
It's not easy to lie low when there's nothing to hide behind!
Flying fish, however, can soar out of the ocean and glide through the air for an incredible 655 feet (200 m) to escape.

A loan shark!

I LIKE TO MOVE IT, MOVE IT!

Many marine mammals travel huge distances to breed or find food. This is called *migration*. Let's get the data on these spectacular swim-a-thons!

Why does an animal migrate?
Usually to breed, give birth, or find food. **Baleen whales** travel from warm breeding grounds in winter to cold feeding areas in summer. The **leatherback turtle** migrates in search of jellyfish, and the **northern elephant seal** completes a double migration every year, first to breed and give birth, and then to shed its fur coat.

Where do sharks go to watch movies?

the dive-in!

How do these animals find their way? Do they have a map?
No! Clever dolphins navigate using **echolocation**, a process in which they map out the ocean floor by sending out clicks and listening to how far the sound travels. Some eels navigate by detecting the strength and direction of the Earth's magnetic field. Scientists also think that the strange noises that whales make might help them remember their routes.

Does migrating marine life get a helping hand when traveling?
Yes, with the **Gulf Stream**! This is a powerful, warm current in the Atlantic Ocean that starts in the Gulf of Mexico, then travels towards Europe and the African coast. In places, it flows 300 times faster than the Amazon River! Animals hitch a ride on this fast-flowing highway.

What mileage do the migrating marine creatures clock up?
Check out these long-distance title holders!

BLUE MARLIN
How far did it travel?
One specimen was tagged near Delaware, then swam to the southeast coast of Africa. That's a respectable 9,254 miles (14,893 km)!

GREAT WHITE SHARK
How far did it travel?
One shark nicknamed Nicole crossed the Indian Ocean twice, clocking in an impressive 12,400 miles (19,956 km)!

LEATHERBACK TURTLE
How far did it travel?
This ancient fellow migrates in search of jellyfish and to lay eggs on the shoreline. Its personal best is 12,700 miles (20,509 km).

ELEPHANT SEAL
How far did it travel?
This seal journeys to the Pacific Ocean twice a year. Males travel 13,000 miles (20,921 km) while females travel 11,000 miles (18,000 km). They all feed in the open ocean to build up energy reserves for their 2-to-4-month fasts on land.

EASTERN PACIFIC GRAY WHALE
How far did it travel?
This migrating machine has gone an epic 14,000 miles (22,531 km) from its Arctic feeding grounds to the Baja lagoons in Mexico.

GO WITH THE FLOW

Our world would be a very different place without plankton! What are these microscopic organisms that are essential to life on Earth? Let's find out!

What is plankton?
Plankton are organisms that can be found floating in almost any body of water on the planet, flowing with the currents, tides, and waves.

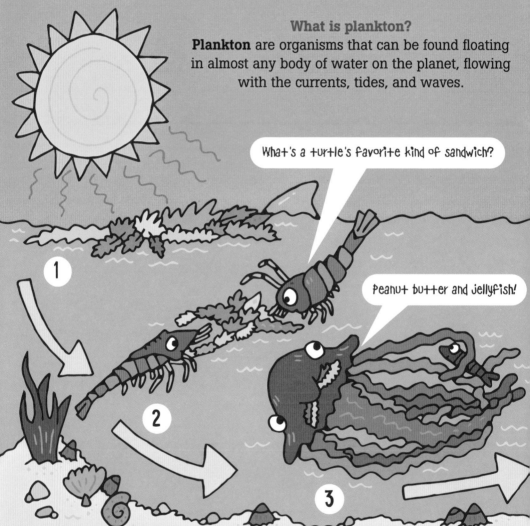

What's a turtle's favorite kind of sandwich?

Peanut butter and jellyfish!

Is plankton a plant or an animal?
Both! There are two main types. **Phytoplankton** (or algae) are plants, and **zooplankton** are animals. Some are too small to be seen by the naked eye, and others, such as krill and jellyfish, can easily be spotted.

Why is plankton so important?
Breathe in! 50% of the oxygen you inhaled was created by phytoplankton. Also, phytoplankton is a crucial component of the food chain.

Hold on! What's a food chain?

It's who eats what and who eats who! When it comes to the ocean and plankton's place in it, here's an example of a food chain:

1. The sun gives the phytoplankton energy.

2. The zooplankton grazes the phytoplankton.

3. Small zooplankton are eaten by larger zooplankton, such as jellyfish.

4. The jellyfish is hunted by the loggerhead turtle.

5. Right at the top of the chain is the tiger shark, who dines on the turtle.

Plankton are handy to have around at the end of the food chain too, as they help break down dead plant and animal material.

Are all phytoplankton planet-friendly?

I'm afraid not. Stay clear of algal blooms, which happen when phytoplankton grow out of control. Some of these colonies of algae are toxic to shellfish, marine mammals, fish, birds, and even humans, and others eat up all the oxygen in the water.

DEEP SEA DISCOVERIES

An incredible 95% of the ocean remains unexplored. What missions are scientists undertaking, and what tools do they use?

What's the breaking ocean news that's making a splash? Scientists are continually updating their deep-sea statistics and discovering new species.

Let's take a look at just a few.

THE HOODWINKER SUNFISH

This curious-looking creature is a recent discovery by marine biologists. It is the largest bony fish in the world, at over 2 tons. This awkward swimmer of a fish wiggles its two fins to paddle its way through the ocean.

WHITE SHARK CAFÉ

Every year, large numbers of sharks travel thousands of miles to a Colorado-sized patch of open ocean, halfway between Hawaii and Mexico. Why they do this, when there is little food to find there, is a mystery. Scientists have tagged some of these creatures to find out what triggers the trip and what they get up to there.

DEEP SEA THERMAL VENTS

Before their discovery in 1977, we assumed that life needed sunlight to survive, but these volcanic vents on the ocean floor are the setting of a unique, sun-free ecosystem. They pump out water that reaches a temperature of almost 750 degrees Fahrenheit (400 degrees Celsius). Not only that, but this water is also rich with minerals that the local bacteria use to make their own food. This bacteria then becomes food for all sorts of wild and wonderful creatures.

What's on the wish list of a budding scientist?

MARINE ROBOT

These unmanned vehicles collect data from the deep ocean. The Benthic Rover is the size of a small car and can spend up to nine months investigating how changes on the surface of the ocean affect creatures down below.

UNDERWATER DROP CAM

Drop cams, high tech cameras that are sunk into the ocean, can relay video in real time from the ocean floor.

SUBMARINE

Explorers can reach dizzying depths in exploratory subs. Film director James Cameron traveled down 6.8 miles (11 km) in 2 hours and 36 minutes aboard one such sub to investigate Earth's deepest ocean trench. The vessel was equipped with a kit that included a sediment sampler, robotic claw, an underwater vacuum to collect sea creatures, and a 3-D video camera.

FACT OR FICTION

Is there a permanent underwater workshop where scientists can solve some of the ocean's puzzles?

Yes! Scientists can live and work in *Aquarius*, a laboratory 62 feet (18 m) under the surface, anchored off the coast of Florida. It can house up to six sea-loving scientists, who can check out the changing ocean and the condition of coral reefs.

What's on a marine biologist's "to-do" list?
A marine biologist studies the animals, plants, and ecosystems of the ocean. Their day-to-day might include collecting specimens, crunching data, or performing experiments in a laboratory.

What are the hot topics being studied right now?
Three of the top research subjects are environmental issues, underwater photosynthesis, and migration patterns.

Who gets a place in the Marine Research Hall of Fame?

JACQUES-YVES COUSTEAU
What makes him such a legendary ocean explorer?
Cousteau was passionate about the sea and devoted his life to sparking that passion in others. He filmed award-winning documentaries that introduced young ocean enthusiasts to the wonders of life in the deep, created technology that allowed explorers to discover uncharted parts of the ocean, and launched conservation efforts to protect the oceans.

RACHEL CARSON
Why was this ocean expert such a trailblazer?
Carson called attention to the issue of human impact on the planet way back in the 1950s. She is famous for her ground-breaking books on sea life and climate change. Many of her works covered how delicate the balance of Earth's ecosystems is, which helped open people's eyes to the importance of protecting the oceans.

VAMPIRE SQUID

CARL CHUN

What was this marine biologist's famous discovery?

This outstanding German professor of zoology led an expedition in 1898, on a voyage through the Atlantic, Indian, and Southern Oceans. There he discovered a number of mysterious deep-sea species, including the spooky-sounding *Vampyroteuthis infernalis*, or vampire squid.

Why do scuba divers always fall backwards out of the boat?

Because if they fell forwards, they'd still be in the boat!

EUGENIE CLARK

Why was she called the "shark lady"?

One of the earliest female marine biologists, Clark made over 70 submarine and scuba dives to study marine life. Prior to her career, people thought sharks were dim-witted and violent animals, but Clark's research and efforts to educate the public helped sharks shake their bad reputation. This phenomenal scientist completed her last dive at the age of 92!

DIVING DOWN TO THE DIZZYING DEPTHS

We're taking a leap into the unknown, where very few humans have ever been. Next stop...the bottom of the ocean!

Where is the deepest point on the planet?
You'll find it in the Pacific Ocean, east of the Philippines. It's a crescent-shaped canyon called the **Mariana Trench**, and it measures a mind-blowing 1,500 miles (2,414 km) long and 43 miles (69 km) wide.

How far down does the trench go?
The deepest part of the Mariana Trench is called **Challenger Deep**, named after the survey ship whose crew tried to take the first measurement of its depth in the 1870s. This spot is...drumroll... over 36,000 feet (10,973 m) down!

Wow! That's hard to imagine! How deep is that?
Slice off Mount Everest at sea level and sink it to the bottom of Challenger Deep. You're now going to make an exhausting 29,000-foot (8,839 m) climb to the top of the mountain. Now look up—you've still got to swim upwards for over a mile (1.6 km) to break the surface of the sea!

What challenges do creatures have to overcome down there?
On land, air presses down on our bodies at 14.5 pounds per square inch. At the bottom of the ocean, water presses down at an eye-popping 15,750 pounds per square inch. The near-freezing water temperatures add to the hostile environment. Marine animals must adapt to avoid being crushed or frozen.

How does the food chain work in the ocean depths?

Lack of sunlight means edible plant life is not an option. Some deep-sea creatures rely on decomposing scraps that float down from the ocean's upper layers. Creatures that live around ocean vents develop the ability to convert chemicals into energy, or feed off creatures who do this.

Can deep-sea inhabitants see in the dark?

Sort of! Marine creatures have adapted to the gloom in different ways. The **tripodfish** uses only touch and vibration to hunt and catch incoming prey. Other species give off their own light that others can see. When it's under attack, the **Atolla jellyfish** gives off a dazzling light display that can be seen 300 feet (91 m) away. This may be an alarm system used to attract an even bigger predator that might grab hold of the Atolla's attacker, letting the jellyfish escape.

Despite inhospitable conditions, the deep ocean is home to an assortment of alien-looking specimens. Shall we shed some light on these curious creatures?

What is this extraordinary exhibit?
It's the **barreleye fish**!

What makes it special?
It has a transparent head, with tubular eyes. These remarkable eyes let the fish look directly upwards, catching sight of potential prey above.

Who is this freaky-looking fish?
It's called an **anglerfish**!

Is that a fishing rod on the top of its head?
Well, kind of! It's an extension of its spine, with a tip of shining flesh. This light attracts unsuspecting prey, which is gulped down by the hungry anglerfish.

Is that a shark I can spot in the deep ocean?
Yes! It's called the **goblin shark**. This specimen is referred to as a "living fossil," as it's related to a 125-million-year-old shark species.

How does the goblin shark hunt in the dark?
Its snout is lined with natural sensors called **ampullae**, which detect weak electrical fields from living creatures. The shark simply tracks down its prey, opens its retractable jaws, and…*chomp*!

Why did the fish blush?

Because it saw the ocean's bottom!

Who is this fang-tastic fellow?
It's the **viperfish**, a real ocean oddball!

What are its distinguishing features?
A viperfish's terrifying teeth are so long they can't even fit in its mouth!

CHILL OUT!

We're paddling to the freezing North Pole and South Pole to get the inside scoop on life among the icebergs.

Wait, are there oceans under all that ice and snow?
Yes! The **Arctic Ocean** is centered around the North Pole and is the world's smallest and shallowest ocean. Much of the ocean is covered in shifting sea ice, with water freezing at 28.8 degrees Fahrenheit (-1.8 degrees Celsius). The **Southern** or **Antarctic Ocean** surrounds Antarctica, home of the South Pole. Chilly sea temperatures there range from 28 to 50 degrees Fahrenheit (-2 to 10 degrees Celsius).

How do marine creatures survive in such cool conditions?
Although the poles get little to no sunlight in winter, the days are long and bright in summer, with the sun never setting for a few weeks each year. Phytoplankton use the 24-hour sunlight to kick into action, nourishing the food chain for a whole year! Larger animals can prevent heat loss by closing off the blood vessels to their feet and flippers and redirecting the warm blood to the middle of their bodies.

Shall we dive into the freezing depths and meet some of Earth's icy survivors?

Name: **NARWHAL** (known as the unicorn of the sea)

How big is it? It weighs 1.5 tons and is 20 feet (6 m) long.

Where is it found? Arctic Ocean

Does it have any distinguishing features?
The male narwhal grows a tooth into a spear-like spiral tusk, measuring nearly 9 feet (2.7 m) long. We're a little unsure about the tusk's purpose. It could be used to find food, to spot a mate, or to detect changes in sea temperature.

Name: ICEFISH (No prizes for guessing how it got its name!)

How big is it? About 30 inches (76 cm)

Where is it found? Southern Ocean

What's its secret weapon? The icefish has antifreeze proteins that pump through its body, helping it to tolerate temperatures below 29 degrees Fahrenheit (-1.7 degrees Celsius).

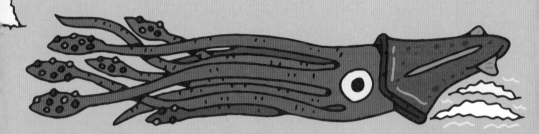

Name: COLOSSAL SQUID

How big is it? Up to 46 feet (14 m) long

Where is it found? The Southern Ocean, at depths of over 3,000 feet (914 m)

How does it see in the dark depths? It has enormous dinner plate-sized eyes, with built-in light organs.

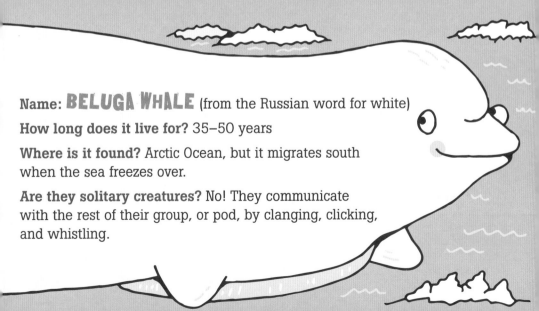

Name: BELUGA WHALE (from the Russian word for white)

How long does it live for? 35–50 years

Where is it found? Arctic Ocean, but it migrates south when the sea freezes over.

Are they solitary creatures? No! They communicate with the rest of their group, or pod, by clanging, clicking, and whistling.

Name: POLAR BEAR

Where does it live? Arctic Sea

How does it swim? It paddles with its large front paws and can close its nostrils when underwater. Its thick layer of fat keeps it warm in the icy ocean.

What does it feed on? It hunts seals and hovers around ice cracks and breathing holes, waiting for its prey to surface.

Are all polar bears white? They're not white at all! Their fur is made from clear, air-filled tubes. These tubes look white to the human eye.

Name: WALRUS

How big is it? It grows up to 11.5 feet (3.5 m), and is twice as heavy as a cow.

Where is it found? Arctic Ocean

What are its tusks used for? These 3-foot (91 cm) long tusks are oversized teeth! The walrus uses them to heave itself out of the cold water and to crack breathing holes in the ice.

What does it eat? Its favorite snacks, shellfish, are located on the ocean floor. In the darkness, a walrus can detect the location of these morsels with its sensitive whiskers.

Name: EMPEROR PENGUIN

How big is it? 3.75 feet (1 m), about the same as an average 6-year-old.

Where is it found? Southern Ocean

How do they keep warm? Penguins have an insulating layer of body fat, multiple rows of waterproof feathers, and an entire flock to huddle with.

How does an emperor penguin swim? They have an aerodynamic body and super-strong flippers. They can reach speeds of up to 7 miles per hour (11 kmph) and make dives that are almost twice the height of the Eiffel Tower.

Are these penguins actually emperors? No, but they are the biggest penguins alive today!

Name: CRABEATER SEAL (They don't eat crabs though!)

Where does it live? Southern Ocean

How big is it? 8.5 feet (2.6 m) long, and it's half as heavy as a grand piano.

What does it eat? Krill. It has special teeth that lets it strain krill from seawater, a little like baleen whales.

Are they an endangered species? Luckily, no! It's estimated that there are 15 to 40 million crabeater seals in the world.

RENT-A-WRECK

With nearly three million shipwrecks on the sea bed, what happens when a wreck comes to rest on the ocean floor?

How does a sunken ship become part of the ocean environment?
In warm water, it can turn into an artificial reef. The wreck is an ideal landing ground for coral polyps, who build their reefs on the ship's hard surfaces. In no time at all, the ship is coated in coral, with fish and other marine life joining them soon after.

What happens if a ship sinks in cold water?
Instead of coral, the wrecks become carpeted with algae, barnacles, sea stars, and mussels. Sunken vessels provide daytime hiding places for crabs and lobsters, who spend their nights searching the wreck for food.

What do divers take to bed?

A snore-kel!

How do some shipwrecks rot away?
Saltwater and oxygen eat away at metal and help turn steel ships into rust. Higher levels of oxygen are found in shallow water, so the deeper a wreck sinks, the better. Any wood or rope is often eaten away by creatures such as shipworms and gribbles.

What is the ocean's most famous shipwreck?

I'm sure you've heard of the *Titanic*. This ship was advertised in 1912 as being "unsinkable," but that proved incorrect when it hit an iceberg in the Atlantic and sank in less than three hours. The wreck of the *Titanic* was discovered in two parts in 1985.

Have any treasure ships been uncovered?

The wreck of the 19th-century Spanish warship *Nuestra Señora de las Mercedes* was a lucky find in 2007, as it contained $500 million in gold that was turned over to the Spanish government.

Is it true that Blackbeard's pirate ship has been discovered?

It's true! The *Queen Anne's Revenge* was found a mile (1.6 km) from North Carolina's Atlantic Beach. Divers have unearthed cannons, weapons, and bags of makeshift ammunition.

FACT
OR
FICTION

43

THE ESSENTIAL OCEAN

A healthy ocean means a healthy planet. Let's show our gratitude for the crucial role the ocean plays in everyone's well-being.

How much food does the ocean supply?
In 2015 alone, commercial fishermen (the people who catch fish sold in supermarkets) hauled in over 9.7 billion pounds of seafood. People who fish for fun caught an additional 351 million fish. That's enough to feed everyone on Earth over a pound of fish a day!

What does the ocean do to help the Earth's atmosphere?
We know that phytoplankton provide 50% of the planet's oxygen. Did you also know that the ocean has absorbed nearly half the carbon dioxide produced by humans in the last 200 years? Phytoplankton helps to keep this gas out of the air, reducing global warming and climate change.

How does the ocean help control the planet's temperatures?
The top layer of the ocean takes in half the heat that the Earth picks up from the sun. This heat is distributed around the world through the ocean's currents, balancing the climate in each continent.

Our crops need rain as well as warm weather. Do the oceans help with this too?

Of course! Water rises up from the surface of the ocean as vapor. When this water vapor meets cold air it forms clouds and rain.

What other natural resources do the oceans provide?
We drill the sea bed to find oil and natural gas. The oil is used in our cars, trucks, and planes, and in plastics and chemicals. We heat our homes with gas, and we use it to cook our food and make steel and glass.

What could the oceans help us with in the future?
Medicine! Coral, sponges, starfish, and seaweed are just a few creatures that scientists study to develop new drugs and antibiotics.

What are some of the major issues affecting the ocean?
For one, we catch fish quicker than they can reproduce, which also means their predators have less to eat. This might result in some species becoming extinct. Abandoned fishing gear is a major problem too, as sea life gets snared in discarded nets.

How does pollution affect the ocean?
Because of the large amount of carbon dioxide being pumped into the atmosphere, the ocean's temperature and acidity has risen. Today, oceans are 25% more acidic than they were before the 19th century, which has been disastrous for marine life. Coral reefs bleach when surrounded by warmer acidic water, and krill numbers drop, which affects the food chain.

How much of our garbage ends up in the ocean?
There are a shocking 5.25 trillion pieces of plastic junk in the ocean. For example, between Hawaii and California you'd find the **Great Pacific Garbage Patch**. This is an 80,000-ton floating island of plastic debris twice the size of Texas. There are currently four other, similarly large ocean-going garbage areas polluting our planet.

Why is plastic such a problem?

Plastic doesn't rot like paper or food, so it remains in the environment for hundreds of years. Sea creatures often mistake plastic bags for jellyfish and eat them. Microplastics, tiny bits of plastic that come from a variety of sources, are so small that they make it through the water filter systems and out to sea. Here they end up in the food chain after being eaten by fish and seabirds.

What are we doing about all of this?

For starters, 4% of the world's oceans are now protected to safeguard the environment. We are setting fishing limits to protect specific species, and the pressure is on for a worldwide ban on plastic bags and cosmetic microbeads.

OPERATION OCEAN CLEAN-UP

We've all got a part to play in preserving the planet. What steps can you take to look after our awesome oceans?

What can I do to use less energy?
Switch off the lights, and take the stairs instead of an elevator. Put on a sweater rather than turning up the heat, and try walking with your folks instead of using a car.

How can I use less plastic?
If you're going to the store, take a cloth bag. If you're going to play sports, fill up a reusable water bottle. Recycle, too!

What can I do to help marine life?
When you're eating out or grabbing groceries, pick out sustainable seafood. If you're on a trip to the beach, tidy up your trash, and try not to take home any rocks, shells, or coral.

How can I work to prevent some species from becoming extinct?
Don't buy products that use materials from a turtle (tortoiseshell), shark, whale, or coral.

Above all, keep reading about life on Earth. The more you learn about the oceans and our phenomenal planet, the more you'll want to protect it!

CHECK OUT ALL OF THE FANTASTIC FACTS IN THIS SENSATIONAL SERIES!

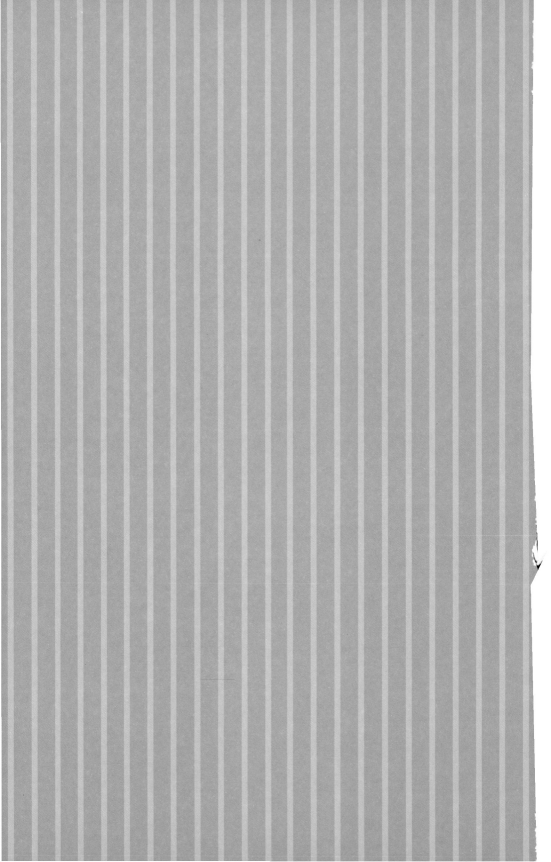